Don't Deliberate... Litigate!

by
Les Abromovitz, Attorney-at-Law

Cover and Inside Illustrations by Darren Thompson.

Published in Glendale Heights, IL by Great Quotations Publishing Co.

Printed in Hong Kong.

DISCLAIMER
(The lawyers have insisted that a book with tongue-in-cheek legal advice requires a disclaimer!)

Kindly note that this publication is not designed to provide accurate and authoritative information in regard to the subject matter covered. It is sold with the understanding that the publisher is not engaged in rendering legal, accounting, or professional service. If legal advice or expert assistance is required, the service of a competent professional person should be sought, which obviously leaves out the attorney who wrote this book.

ACKNOWLEDGEMENTS

I owe a great deal of thanks to my wife, Hedy, who's put up with me for twenty years without once threatening to sue. Special thanks go to my family who will never ask me to handle any legal matters again after reading this book. Besides, I've done enough damage already. And, finally I'm grateful to Susanne of Great Quotations who's been supportive, fun to work with, and diplomatic, all of which you'd never expect from an editor.

Table of Contents

Chapter One

Suits Ahoy

We are in the midst of a litigation explosion. Lawsuits are being initiated in record numbers. We are in an era where suits are brought to resolve the most trivial problems or to compensate the most insignificant injuries. The thoughtful person will ask what he or she can do. After consideration of all the issues, the obvious answer is to jump aboard the litigation bandwagon.

At first, the notion of bringing a lawsuit at the drop of a hat will seem distasteful. Many may resist the idea as being a monumental hassle and an unethical waste of our society's resources. A thorough analysis, however, will reveal that the financial rewards and personal satisfaction outweigh any of the disadvantages.

It is every American's right to clog the courts with nonsensical lawsuits. Besides, if your attorney doesn't have any ethical qualms about bringing a lawsuit that's without merit, why should you? It's time you stopped being litigiously-impaired.

There are suits ahoy, matey, so happy suing.

You can sue a state trooper who refuses to grade your sobriety test on a curve.

Show your secretary who's boss. Sue her for age discrimination if she won't date you because you're an old fart, not to mention married. And to show her there are no hard feelings, buy her the Wonderbra for Secretary's Day.

Sue the bastards who make fun of your rug... I mean, hairpiece. While you're at it, sue people who've given you bad directions.

A lawsuit can put an end to a priest's nebbing into your private affairs. It's immaterial that he was hearing your confession. Furthermore, asking you to do penance violates the constitutional prohibition against cruel and unusual punishment. You can sue a rabbi whose sermon runs too long. File the papers and watch him say "Oy!"

Everyone hates insurance companies, so you can't lose by suing. You can sue the insurance company that cancels your auto policy, just because you got liquored up and smashed the day care center van. Isn't that what insurance is for?

File suit against your plastic surgeon, if you still can't find work after the implants.

You can sue a hotel if you're forced to get your own peanuts and drinks from the in-room mini-bar. Every mini-bar must have a bartender. While your attorney is drawing up the papers, sue guests in the next hotel room who moan too loudly during foreplay and cause you sexual frustration. You can collect even more, if it's your spouse.

You can sue a lifeguard for not letting you go down for the third time Better to drown than to die from embarrassment. Don't forget to name *Dionne Warwick and the Psychic Friends Network* for failing to warn you of the danger.

You don't have to be a hand model to sue for paper cuts. Whether it's your employer, the paper manufacturer, the store you bought it in, or the logger who felled the tree, you can sue for pain and suffering, as well as disfigurement.

If your movie theater serves fattening popcorn, sue for the increased risk of heart disease you're likely to encounter. The theater is also liable, if the on-screen nudity doesn't meet your expectations because the star's been eating too much of the popcorn.

Chapter Two

DEFENSE

History of the Litigation Explosion

Most people think the litigation explosion is a new phenomenon, brought about by the recent influx of greedy lawyers scrounging for business. This perception is an insult to all of the greedy attorneys who have been around for years. In reality, people have been suing in record numbers since the 1950s.

Few people are aware that the Stooges were suing each other on a regular basis. Most of those eye pokes, face slaps and hair pulling resulted in lawsuits. In fact, the Stooges eventually broke up, because no company would insure them.

Another landmark case was against Gilligan and the Skipper by the castaways. It was charged that they were negligent in navigating the S.S. Minnow. Eventually, this case was thrown out, since none of the parties could get off the island to appear in court.

Sexual harassment suits have been commonplace for many years and not just because of the casting couch. Miss Kitty sued Marshall Dillon on several occasions for sexual battery. Each time, however, juries ruled that she was asking for it.

Years later, however, women everywhere applauded the Supreme Court decision which struck a major blow against sexual harassment. Mary Richards successfully sued Ted, Murray, and Lou Grant for making romantic overtures and stalking her at home.

Gomer Pyle is still in court over his discharge from the military because he's gay. Nonetheless, he did successfully sue Sgt. Carter for verbal abuse.

Litigation involving the Clampetts was especially bitter. Jethro and Elly May fought for years over Granny's estate. Jed was named in a palimony suit brought by Miss Hathaway. Mr. Drysdale was sued frequently as a result of his role in the S&L scandal.

Long before the Rodney King case, lawsuits against the police were common. Barney Miller was sued many time for police brutality. Officers Toody and Muldoon eventually had to leave the force, because of civil suits against them.

Even famous lawyer, Perry Mason, was sued by Hamilton Burger, the district attorney, for withholding evidence until trial, thus making him look bad in court. As always, however, Burger lost.

Chapter Three

Torts For Tots

Kids have it tough. They have to depend on their parents for money unless, God forbid, they get a job. The enterprising child will soon realize that litigation is the answer to those cash flow woes.

Nothing instills family values more than a lawsuit. If your parents exposed you to second hand smoke or made you wear second hand clothes, you can cash in on the litigation explosion. Twins, for example, can sue parents who make them dress alike.

The courts have determined that Mom and Dad should be granted no special favors. Even more conservative jurisdictions are stripping away the traditional immunity of parents from suits brought by their children.

The first case of this type was initiated years ago. Adam, Hoss and Little Joe were forced to sue their father, Ben Cartwright, after he failed to pay them for working on the Ponderosa Ranch.

Progressive parents will respect and look with pride at the child who takes them to court. It is a sign that the child is becoming an adult, a ritual almost as sacred as the Bar Mitzvah. When a child threatens parents with a lawsuit, it is a major milestone. Even if you weren't born with a silver spoon in your mouth, you can buy one later by suing your parents.

They're to blame for all your problems, whether they be psychological or physical. Your parents supplied the genes that are causing you to go bald, as well as that honker you call a nose. The answer is as plain as the nose on your face: Sue them.

They're also responsible for your sexual problems. What child wasn't traumatized by walking in on her parents having sex? In fact, the mere thought of their parents having sex has destroyed the act for many people.

And here's another tip. Circumcised males can sue their parents, if they're getting the short end on their sex life.

You can sue your mother, if she opens your mail. Even the unemployed who live at home at age forty have rights.

Parents have a legal obligation to provide more than just the bare necessities of life. They must pay for tutors, so their child will have more free time to watch television and play video games. Parents must pay for more than just college boards. They must also pay for SAT prep courses, as well as a ringer to take these tests for them.

Every child has a right to be in a band. Therefore, parents must pay for music lessons, instruments, and sound equipment. And if they're not musically inclined, every child has the right to sleep with the band.

The right to drive is an inalienable one. Children can't be stripped of these privileges, just because of a few tickets and a fender bender with a police car. A curfew can't be imposed, unless martial law has been declared.

You can sue grandparents who stop sending birthday gifts, just because they haven't gotten a thank you note in seventeen years. There is an implied contract requiring them to send these gifts, no matter how ungrateful their grandchildren are.

Grandparents owe more than just birthday, Christmas, and graduation gifts. An obscure provision of the *Uniform Gift to Minors Act* requires them to fund a custodial account for their offspring. So, if grandpap won't demonstrate his affection with cash, slap a lawsuit on him and watch the old geezer squirm.

The resourceful child can sue his parents or grandparents for squandering their estate by buying luxury items like groceries. Children can seek an injunction, if grandparents start traveling in their sunset years or show any signs of enjoying their retirement, since this might diminish the child's inheritance.

If there's one thing that scares teachers more than a twelve year old with a tatoo, it's the threat of an educational malpractice suit. The first case of this kind was the Sweathogs versus Kotter, but there have been many lawsuits since then.

An educational malpractice suit can keep teachers off your back. Instead of an apple, bring a summons to class. If your report card is bad, sue the teacher for libel. You'll get high marks from your lawyer.

Litigation of this type can be used to force a teacher to grade on a curve or to accept a review of "The Simpsons" for extra credit. Students can allege that negligent teaching methods were the cause of their low grades or that the instructor's evaluation system discriminated against those who didn't attend class. The *Americans With Disabilities Act* states that students with limited attention spans must be given the freedom to roam the halls at will.

A phys-ed teacher can be sued on the grounds that his improper coaching methods caused a student/athlete to lose a multimillion dollar contract. Coaches can be sued for failing to play the third-string center in the big game, thus ruining his chances of getting lucky with any of the cheerleaders.

Sex education teachers can be held financially responsible for unwanted children, since they apparently didn't get their message across to students. They also can be sued, if sex isn't all it's cracked up to be in class. Furthermore, students can sue if the sex in class isn't all it's cracked up to be.

Kids can also sue the school and the school district over the food in the cafeteria. Naturally, you can't sue if the food isn't tasty, because there'd be lawsuits all the time. Nevertheless, children can sue if the food is too hot and they get burned in a food fight.

You can sue the parochial school you attend for failing to offer a course in Yiddish. You can dust off that lawsuit and file it again when you get to Notre Dame.

Children can sue candy manufacturers if their product gives them zits before the prom. Of course, the kids will have to prove it wasn't the seven Domino's pizzas, in which case they can sue them. Their lawyer can be down at the courthouse in thirty minutes or less.

The image of a weak and helpless child is a distorted one. There is an army of lawyers out there, ready to give kids some muscle. What better way to expedite the maturation process than by letting them handle matters the adult way-through the litigation process.

Lawsuits are a panacea for all the problems of growing up. Above all, children must learn that the threat of a lawsuit is a socially acceptable form of extortion. Tantrums are kid stuff; lawsuits are the adult method of getting your way.

Chapter Four

Suing
Relatives & Friends

Torts aren't just for tots. They're for any family, except for a deviant few.

You've seen them in restaurants and they're absolutely sickening. There are twelve of them from several generations, laughing and hugging at the next table. It's like the Waltons are having breakfast. They're so wholesome, it makes you want to gag. Watching that transpire is especially nauseating, if you and your relatives can't make it through a family dinner without suing one another.

Unless you come from one of those sick families that get along, suing a relative can be a dream come true. And it's really beneficial to the family unit in the long run. Right now, when family members get angry, they stop talking to one another for years. With a lawsuit, as soon as the case is resolved, you're one big happy family again.

The first case of this kind occurred in the early 1970s when Mike sued Archie Bunker after being called "Meathead" once too often. Although Bunker paid a sizable settlement, he is doing well financially, having married Marge Schott after Edith's death.

If you come from a big family, you'll have plenty of relatives to sue. In a landmark case, Chip, Robbie, Mike and Ernie sued Uncle Charley for making them do the dishes one too many times. You can sue your Dad's brother and make him say "uncle."

Don't overlook your aunt whose cooking is always making you sick. Before her death, Andy sued Aunt Bea on countless occasions for that reason.

Similarly, you can sue relatives for slander, if they bad-mouth you. Think of it. You'll get rich from just your mother-in-law alone.

Or how about your brother who's always picked on you, not to mention his being more successful. Remember all of those pillow fights? You can sue for assault.

Unless you come from a small family, suing relatives is relatively easy. When it comes to suing friends though, the sky's the limit. You can never have enough friends. Every friend means another potential lawsuit.

In another era, people didn't sue their friends. Otherwise, Beaver Cleaver would have been suing Eddie Haskell after every episode. If he had, however, things might have turned out better for Beaver who later died in Viet Nam and for Eddie who went on to become a police officer in Los Angeles.

Nevertheless, there have been notable cases throughout the years. Fred Flintstone sued Barney Rubble for running off with Wilma, charging alienation of affection.

For years, your friends have been giving you advice. When the advice didn't turn out well, your only option was to throw it up to them forever. A lawsuit is a more lucrative way to make them sorry for butting into your personal affairs.

You can sue your neighbors, if you get overheated in their jacuzzi. If they didn't want you using it, they should have built a higher fence. This is an attractive nuisance and entitles you to become an unattractive nuisance in court.

A true friend won't desert you after a lawsuit. He or she will recognize that business is business and it's nothing personal. Your real friends will understand that it's your only way to make a buck, especially in view of your limited career possibilities. Buy them a beer to show there are no hard feelings.

Chapter Five

A Man, a Woman, and Their Attorney

You might have noticed that we've left out a very important relative you can sue. That's right—your spouse. The cases permitting suits by children against their parents were landmark decisions. Because husbands and wives have battled each other for years in courtrooms across the land, it was not unexpected when judges abolished interspousal immunity and permitted suits between them.

Years ago, suits like these were thrown out of court. For example, Rob Petrie once tried to sue his wife, Laura, after tripping over the ottoman in the entryway.

Public policy demands that suits between spouses be allowed. Marriages are preserved, because couples have a more amicable forum in which to resolve their differences. Furthermore, these lawsuits reduce a couple's money problems, which we all know is a leading cause of marital difficulties.

By allowing these suits, the marital contract can be interpreted by learned judges who have vast experience in these matters, having watched their own marriages dissolve. The judge can force spouses to fulfill their marital obligations. As an example, if a woman gets dry heaves from having sex with her husband, she can be forced to perform her wifely duties. While court orders are the most appropriate method for compelling performance, a husband can use a stun gun or tranquilizer darts to assure compliance.

* Note: Despite heavy lobbying by the National Rifle Association, assault weapons are not permitted unless there is a seven day waiting period.

When a couple has sexual problems, it is often difficult to know who's at fault. Many bar associations have promulgated rules, forbidding sex between attorneys and clients. Therefore, it is up to judges to sample the merchandise and make a decision. Once again, a lawsuit is far better alternative to a divorce action.

You can sue your spouse's vibrator for alienation of affection. While you're at it, sue the models in *PLAYBOY* and *PLAYGIRL* for alienation of affection, if your spouse spends the day drooling over them. You can sue your spouse for drooling over your furniture. It's half yours, you know.

You can sue a spouse who bites your head off. Pre-menstrual syndrome (PMS) is a defense, however. For men, an overtime loss in any game is also a defense.

File a lawsuit against your spouse, if she isn't amorous at three in the morning when you get home from the bar. It's not like she can't go back to sleep until six. Besides, it's only two minutes out of her day, so what's the big deal?

You can sue newlyweds and young people, who make your sexual performance look inadequate. While you're at the courthouse, sue your spouse who knows for a fact that your sexual performance is inadequate.

Unfortunately, there are gray areas in the law. Suppose your husband won't indulge you by wearing that tool belt and handyman outfit. Or perhaps, your snotty feminist wife finds it degrading to wear that Frederick's of Hollywood chambermaid costume or that present from Garters-R-Us. This is obviously a matter for the courts to decide. A jury of twelve reasonable men and women should decide if these outfits offend their sense of decency. Even if you lose, keep tabs on which jurors weren't offended by these garments and give them a call later.

Litigation can make you rich and improve your sex life.

Now that suits between spouses are permitted, you can recover for all of the injuries you once thought were insignificant. A man can sue his wife, if her cooking gives him indigestion. A wife can sue her husband, if he fails to maintain the car in good mechanical condition and it breaks down. Litigation can be used to enforce these sexual stereotypes.

After the marital ties have been severed, litigation can still play a role in helping the parties put their lives back together. Both parties will adjust better to the custody arrangement, if they're aware of the legal consequences of their acts. For example, you can't just call your children and mention that you divorced their mother, because she wanted to leave them in the woods with the dingoes. Statements like these can only be made during the prescribed visitation hours. In addition, you can use weight charts to show your former spouse is an unfit parent.

The most bitter custody disputes, however, revolve around pets. It is often in the best interest of the pet for the family to resolve these matters amicably. Otherwise, it will be subjected to a battery of psychological tests. Furthermore, being forced to choose between the husband or wife will often traumatize these innocent victims of divorce.

Attorneys have always known that it's wrong for two incompatible people to stay together. There's no money in it. The real money is in bitter divorces where couples fight over property and custody for years.

Courtrooms give couples the opportunity to air their differences. They also give them a chance to air their dirty linen in public. Remember that no matter is too petty or too personal for the legal system to handle.

Chapter Six

DEFENSE

Sic Your Lawyer on Your Employer

There is nothing that will ingratiate you more with prospective employers than leashing your attorney on them. Employers respect that in an applicant. It shows them that the applicant is aggressive and won't take any crap.

Some job applicants like to take an attorney along with them to the interview. While this is a nice touch to be sure, it's enough to just threaten a lawsuit during the interview. This will prevent illegal questions, like why you have a skull and crossbones tatooed on your face.

In most cases, suing is better than working. If a rejection letter promises to hold your resume on file for six months, you can show up with a court order and make surprise inspections.

Charge prospective employers with discrimination in their hiring practices. In your case, they're discriminating against people who've been fired from their last seven jobs.

Some employers discriminate on the basis of achievement, which is blatantly unlawful. Courts have ruled this would show bias toward overachievers and people who graduated high school. Your experience serving Big Gulps should not be valued any less than a Ph.D or specific experience in the job field.

When a judge orders the company to give you a job, you'll have the opportunity to prove what a valuable employee you are. Soon, you'll be on your way to upper management with no hard feelings on either side.

Once you do land a job, you have to be prepared to sue to protect your rights. If you make a decision to be freeze-dried because of a terminal illness, your employer must hold your job open for you.

You can't lose your job as a truck driver, just because of that accident with a school bus. Where would this country be, if you have to worry about losing your job every time you fall asleep at the wheel?

If you are fired unlawfully, the wrongful discharge suit is your remedy. The first case of this kind was George Jetson versus Spacely Sprockets. Although Jetson won his case, he got into trouble later for failing to pay Social Security taxes on Rosie, his maid's, wages.

Litigation can give you the leverage you need to keep your job, despite your performance. Suppose your boss interferes with your forty-five minute bathroom break. It's implied in the Constitution that employers can't disrupt your daily constitutional. In fact, the First Amendment obligates employers to supply reading matter of your choice.

There are a number of civil actions that can be utilized against an unreasonable manager. If she comments unfavorably about your performance, sue for defamation. A false imprisonment action is available, if she demands overtime or makes you work through lunch.

Your boss is required to respect your seniority rights. If you're a busboy with the most seniority and a position as chef becomes available, you must be promoted to that job. Similarly, if you are the orderly with the longest tenure at a hospital, you can demand any neurosurgeon jobs that come open.

Suppose your boss gives you a hard time, just because you're working on your side business on company time and using their supplies. It's a violation of the antitrust laws for the employer to curtail your activities, since this is a restraint of trade.

Your co-workers can be kept in line too. Suppose all of them are working at a speed which makes your production totals look sickly. In fact, you have the lowest output in the company, despite your obvious intellectual superiority. This situation can be rectified with an action for intentional infliction of emotional distress. Before long, those co-workers will be working at a rate which isn't so ungodly.

You can sue a co-worker who wins the employee-of-the-month award that's rightfully yours. You would have won it, had you not called in sick for twelve straight days.

Take your employer to court, if he won't let you bring your Uzi to work. This violates your Fourth Amendment right to bear arms. You may not, however, supply an Uzi to Smokey or Gentle Ben, because there is no constitutional right to arm bears.

You do, however, have a constitutional right to smoke. Therefore, you can sue an employer who implements a no-smoking policy. There is no reason why a Coronary Care nurse shouldn't be allowed to light up. If this incursion on civil liberties is tolerated, smoke breaks might be limited one day to five an hour.

You can bring a lawsuit against an employer who prohibits porno magazines in the workplace. Even prisoners get conjugal visits.

You can sue an employer who fires you, simply because you got the company indicted as a result of your stupidity. Firing someone for stupidity violates the *Americans With Disabilities Act.*

Lawyers should have job security too. You can sue the law firm that fired you, just because you stole a few bucks from clients. You would have gotten around to paying it back eventually. It's not like that elderly widow even noticed it was missing.

You can sue your employer, if the company won't let you dance on the job. Dancing is a form of self-expression and prohibiting it violates the First Amendment. (See Kevin Bacon versus John Lithgow in "Footloose" for legal guidance.) In a recent case, a mortuary employee won $700,000 and got his job back, after being fired for dancing on the job. The court made it clear, however, that dancing on someone's grave would be prohibited.

You don't have to die to sue an employer who's working you to death. It is unconstitutional to require American workers to put in a full day's work for a full day's pay.

Above all, remember that an employer can't replace you and pretend that nothing is different. This legal principle was upheld in the case of the Two Darrens versus Bewitched.

You don't have to be a lawyer to make your living in the courtroom. Once you start collecting on lawsuits, you won't need to sue your employer. In fact, you won't need to be employed ever again. Call in sick and head for the courthouse.

Chapter Seven

Malpractice
Makes Perfect

It would make little sense to talk about professional malpractice. After all, you probably can't afford to see a doctor, so suing for medical malpractice is out of the question for now. Besides, if you're a typical American, you've already filed at least ten medical malpractice cases by your thirtieth birthday. What you really need is to know more about the innovative forms of medical malpractice.

You'd be nuts not to sue your psychiatrist or psychologist. Bob Newhart was sued frequently by his patients. Eventually, he had to leave his practice and buy an inn in Vermont.

Since you probably need a psychiatrist but can't afford one, let's start with a suit against your radio psychologist. Suppose Dr. Grant's four minute analysis of your problem can't correct thirty years of psychological damage. In her life script, she'll be reading a lawsuit from you.

Dr. Ruth is not immune from litigation either. Let's say you misunderstand her sexual advice because of that thick German accent and make a fool out of yourself with your next bed partner. You can sue for the damage to your ego. If you can bring witnesses to testify that your sexual technique has not improved as a result of following her advice, you will be orgasmic at the size of the verdict.

Members of the clergy are not sacrosanct. You can sue them for any bad advice they give you. Let's take a common example. Your minister advises you not to run away with the fourteen year old clerk at the video store and suggests that you stay with your wife and six children. Soon thereafter, the girl wins the lottery and you lose out on a million dollars. Suing your minister will sooth the hurt he caused you. And if your conscience bothers you, throw an extra ten in the collection plate.

Suing an accountant is just as rewarding. Notice I didn't say "your" accountant, since you probably don't have one. To save a few bucks, you asked a woman at work whose brother is a CPA to answer a tax question. She asks her brother, but the answer gets a little jumbled in the translation. As a result, your tax problem gets worse, thanks to that poor excuse for an accountant. Balance the books by suing him for malpractice.

Better yet, sue the woman for malpractice. Intermediaries who relay questions to professionals are held responsible for their acts. Using this precedent, you can sue anyone related to a professional.

As an example, you can sue a plumber whose cousin is a physician, if he gives you bad medical advice. Relatives of physicians take an oath to answer any and all medical questions for people who don't want to shell out money for a doctor. They are held accountable for any bad medical advice that they give.

When all else fails, you can always extract money from your dentist. Hasn't she been harassing you with those, postcards, telling you it's time for a checkup? Didn't she humiliate you by criticizing your flossing technique and by implying that your dental hygiene left a lot to be desired? Isn't your orthodontist responsible for your son using his retainer as a nose ring? It's time to put your attorney on retainer and sink your teeth into a juicy malpractice suit.

Chapter Eight

The Humorless
Consumer

Disappointed consumers have been suing companies for decades, when a product or service doesn't live up to their expectations.

People who bring products liability lawsuits owe a debt of gratitude to the Road Runner. His suits against the Acme Company have paved the way for all consumers.

Misuse of the product is no obstacle to success either. The case of Popeye versus DelMonte clearly illustrates that even if you open a can of spinach by squeezing it until the top pops off, the company is responsible if your hand is cut.

If you choose to use your shower massage as a paint sprayer, the manufacturer is legally obligated to anticipate that contingency and manufacture the product accordingly. For example, a consumer may absent-mindedly take his rowing machine out on the lake. Again, the manufacturer should anticipate this occurrence and build flotation devices into the rowing mechanism.

Products liability law permits suits against against any party involved in the manufacturing or distribution of the rowing machine. With sophisticated word processing equipment, 112 of the Fortune 500 can be sued with little difficulty. Don't forget the company that made the rubber tips to protect the carpet. They could have made them out of a buoyant material. If they're not at fault, let them prove it.

As a consumer, there are countless opportunities for litigation. If you still have cellulite, you can sue the author and the book publisher who offered advice on how to lose it. Please note, however, that there must be a contractual relationship between you and the publisher. You must show that you bought the book for 49 cents and didn't simply read it in the supermarket line. Similarly, you can sue if you're listening to an audio book in the car and fall asleep at the wheel.

If you're having a bad hair day, sue the maker of your shampoo. You need a bad hair week, however, to really collect big damages. You can sue a shaving cream manufacturer, if you have five o'clock shadow before five. And women can collect even more.

You can sue the manufacturer, if your inflatable date deflates your ego.

Infomercials will be a breeding ground for future lawsuits. You can sue if your spray-on hair won't come off, even with turpentine, or if you spray it in your eyes.

You can sue the maker of Ginsu knives, if someone robs you with one. They have a duty to make sure these knives don't fall in the wrong hands. If you act quickly, you can sue.

Your failure to read the warning or instruction book is no impediment to a lawsuit. In fact, the consumer who hopes to sue would be wise to ignore the instructions. These directions often contain information that will help you avoid injury. And that's the last thing you need, if you're planning on suing.

Keep in mind that a real injury is a useful, though not indispensable, requirement for a successful lawsuit. Usually, the more severe your injury is, the bigger your verdict will be. The intelligent litigant can never be warned strongly enough. Never be discouraged by a product that seems to be safe. In your hands, any product can be defective and unreasonably dangerous.

Products must contain explicit warnings of their detrimental side effects. Potato chip makers must put a warning on every bag. You must be told in writing that your arteries will become clogged with grease from continued consumption of their chips.

Using the cigarette cases as precedent, you can sue the chip makers on the grounds that their product is addictive and you are unable to stop yourself from eating them. In their ads, they have admitted the addictive quality of potato chips by betting you can't eat just one. Don't walk around with a chip on your shoulder. Make the potato chip manufacturers shoulder the blame for your compulsive eating habits.

That eating disorder can come in handy when you're looking for a lawsuit to file. You can sue an amusement park if the rides make you nauseous. It doesn't matter that you stuffed yourself with cotton candy and nachos all day, because they could have anticipated that you'd pig out on those items.

A trip to the grocery store can lead to a trip to the courthouse. You can sue the store, not to mention the farmer, if you break a denture eating corn. And if you want big money, sue the bagger who gives you paper when you specifically asked for plastic. Don't overlook the checkout person who won't accept your expired coupons.

File a lawsuit against bill collectors who write you nasty letters, just because you're a year or two behind on your bills. You can sue stores that harass you by sending bills, as well as the postman who delivers them. You can sue the bearer of bad news.

Chapter Nine

Lawsuits
of the
Rich &
Famous

It happens all the time. Some nobody sues a celebrity and makes big money. Think of how proud you'd be, if it were you who's doing the suing.

The procedure is a simple one. Pick up one of the tabloids, while you're waiting in the check-out line. You'll see dozens of celebrities you can sue.

As a starting point, ask yourself a simple question: What color hair do I have? If it's black, you can easily claim that you're Elvis' lovechild as so many others have done. If it's red, you can charge that you're Opie Taylor's lovechild. If it's blonde, you can sue and argue that you're MacCaulay Culkin's lovechild.

You get the picture. Though it sounds easy, there are a few precautions you must take. A clever defense lawyer may trap you into admitting what your natural hair color is on the stand. It also helps, if you're younger than MacCaulay Culkin.

If these cases don't suit your fancy, there are dozens of other possibilities. You can sue Michael Bolton on the grounds that he fathered your baby.

Before making these allegations, however, you may wish to consult your husband first. Some men are heavily into this macho thing and might get huffy, just because you're saying someone else is the father of your child.

Better yet, you can accuse that romance novel hunk, Fabio, of fathering your child. Look through those eight thousand romance novels where Fabio appears bare-chested on the cover. One of those heroines next to him must look something like you.

When you find one, you can offer the book as evidence of your relationship with Fabio. It will be fabulous.

Lawsuits like this are more than just a money-making opportunity. It's a great way to meet celebrities. Let's say you're dying to meet Bruce Springsteen. A copyright infringement suit can be the perfect introduction. It's better than a back-stage pass.

Doesn't "Born in the USA" sound a little like that song you wrote on the Kimball organ? Well, except for the cha-cha beat that your song has. It doesn't matter that Springsteen never heard the song. If the resemblance is strong enough or the jury is tone-deaf, you can prove he stole it.

To make your case even stronger, start sending tapes to all of your favorite performers. They'll never be able to write another song without you suing them for copyright infringement. And every record you buy will be royalties in your pocket.

Unfortunately, the artist may settle out-of-court to avoid the expense and publicity of defending the case. And even if you do go to court, some stars have been known to be rude to the parties suing them. It just goes to show what an ego trip these performers are on. Go figure.

These are just a few of the potential lawsuits against the rich and famous. You can also sue those sitcom stars who are so sickeningly sweet, it makes you want to barf. You can sue Richard Simmons if his "Sweating With the Oldies" tape does make you barf but you still don't lose weight. Make Richard sweat with a lawsuit.

Ann Landers and Abigail Van Buren are potential targets too. They are giving out advice every day that could screw up your life. It's a perfect opportunity to sue them, as long as the jury doesn't find out your life was screwed up already. Another problem is that Ann and Abby both died decades ago and the advice is actually being given by Mary Worth.

Another option is to hang out where the celebrities hang out. Then, you can pick a fight or be a royal pain in the ass. Eventually, the celebrity will take a swing at you and there's your lawsuit.

You might not know how to pick a fight. Maybe, you just infuriate people for no apparent reason. When you encounter celebrities, you're not going to be with them long enough to let your obnoxious personality anger them. You'll need to work fast.

The tried-and-true methods aren't enough. Oh sure, you can stalk them when they go out or break into their house, but that won't always work. You can interrupt their dinner out and bother them when they go to the bathroom, but some celebrities are able to tolerate rude behavior. Even "your mama" insults may not provoke an assault. You need something more dramatic.

Try combining that rude behavior with a bad impression of the celebrity. At a key moment in the Laker game, go up to Jack Nicholson and do your imitation of him. He'll go crazy and take a poke at you.

Almost everybody can do a Clint Eastwood impression. Interrupt him on the set with it and watch the sparks fly. Then, go ahead and make his day with a lawsuit.

Let's say you run into Robert DeNiro and want to goad him into a fight. Try this: "Are you looking at me? I don't see anybody else in the room, so you must be looking at me." Within seconds, he'll be ready to wring your neck.

Or suppose you run into Florence Henderson. Go up to her and sing "The Brady Bunch" theme at the top of your lungs. I guarantee she'll go for your throat and you can sue.

With some celebrities, you won't have to do anything to instigate a fight. Unfortunately, however, suing celebrities would be a lot easier if there were more Shannen Dohertys and Sean Penns in Hollywood.

Sports figures are perfect targets too. They are wealthy and volatile. You know they'll be in a bad mood after a tough loss. You also know exactly where to find them before the big game...either in a bar or some groupie's hotel room. It may even be your hotel room, if you play your cards right.

You can sue a sports figure who strikes out, fumbles, misses a free throw, or anything else that causes you to lose a bet. But watch out. Athletes can sue fans who boo, just because they're batting .190 and are making three million a year.

A lawsuit is payback for high ticket prices. If you can't be a free agent, you can at least sue one. Suing celebrities is a way for you to get money and your fifteen minutes of fame. It's the price the rich and famous must pay for being rich and famous.

Chapter Ten

Suing The Airlines: Some Plane Facts

You've waited in long ticket lines and paid outrageously high prices. You've circled the airport for hours and sat endlessly on runways. You've been wronged and it's time for the airlines to right those wrongs.

Oh sure, you'd love to be in an airline disaster and make some real money, but why wait. Litigation is your ticket to exotic places. Start filing lawsuits against the airlines. Give yourself a frequent filer award.

You can sue a flight attendant who rebuffs your advances. It is implied in that ticket contract that flight attendants welcome propositions and an occasional pat on the tuchas. When the flight crew does not enjoy these advances, it should be clearly stated on the ticket in bold print near the warning about lost luggage.

At the very least, you are legally entitled to at least one drop-dead good looking flight attendant. In recent years, the airlines have overlooked physical assets in favor of intelligence and efficiency. You don't have to stand for this. The FAA requires that each flight crew contain one or more former swimsuit calendar model. Otherwise, the wet t-shirt contests just aren't any fun.

When there is new technology, there are also new rules that the airlines must obey or risk a lawsuit. There must be a phone on every plane and that phone must have call waiting.

If rough weather is encountered and the airline refuses to serve food, you can sue them for deprivation of the basic human necessities. If they do serve food in bad weather and someone within nine rows throws up, you can hurl a lawsuit at them. If they won't serve you kosher food, even though you're an agnostic and never requested it in advance, a cause of action arises. Aviation law requires airlines to keep a rabbi aboard every flight in anticipation of this occurrence.

More recent laws stipulate that there be low calorie meals offered on every flight and a fitness center. On flights of two hours or longer, a salad bar must be available. Unless it's a commuter flight, your plane must have a fully-stocked wine cellar. You can request that your meal be prepared at your seat, as long as you ask in advance for this service. Fondue must also be made available, if requested.

Entertainment is legally required on flights too. Along with the requisite safety equipment, planes must carry karaoke machines too. In addition, the First Amendment guarantees that all in-flight movies be uncensored, so that all gratuitous nudity and car chases are kept intact.

There are even a few airlines that for some reason, won't show films that involve airplane crashes. This deprives passengers of wonderful movies like, "Airport," featuring a deeply-moving dramatic performance by Dean Martin.

Despite recent regulations, no airline can restrict your right to smoke. All that's missing is a test case to overturn these blatantly illegal laws. You could go down in the legal treatises as that person, if you're willing to stand up for your rights or can't go another second without a nicotine fix. Next time you're at 35,000 feet, light up. Don't tamper with the smoke detector in the lavatory. Strike a match for freedom and blow smoke in the flight attendant's face. When the flight crew tells you to put it out, just say "no" or "bite me," if that's more your style.

Better yet, pull out a cig in one of those airports with the so-called no-smoking policies. Assert yourself and challenge the ban. The hell with airport security. Eventually, the ban on cigarettes will be declared unconstitutional and you'll collect damages for false arrest.

You also have a constitutional right to drink. This means that you're entitled to drinks. The flight attendants aren't allowed to cut you off either, no matter how many times you've tried to open the emergency exit door for laughs.

Don't just sue the airlines. On every flight, there are hundreds of other possible people to sue, whether it's the passenger in front who puts his bald head in your lap while you're eating or the three-year old who's kicked your seat for seven hours. You may have to wait awhile to collect the judgment against the three-year old, but think of the interest.

It's time you stopped whining about the cost of airfare. Every flight can be a money-maker, if you'll get your head out of the clouds.

Chapter Eleven

Suing
For Your Supper

Eating out can be an expensive proposition. That's been your big mistake. You've been missing out on the opportunities to sue that are present in every restaurant. Each dinner out is a varitable smorgasbord of litigation possibilities.

Have you ever gotten sick after a meal at a restaurant? OK, so maybe it wasn't right after the meal. It might have been a few days later or even a month. In any event, you ate there and you got sick. Since it's too late to stiff the waiter, you need an equally satisfying remedy - the lawsuit.

You've filled your face and your stomach, so it's time to fill your pockets. File a suit against the restaurant and let them prove it wasn't their food that caused your illness. With the money you make, you can become a regular at that same restaurant. Show them there are no hard feelings by patronizing them often and tipping well.

As we've stressed time and time again throughout this book, don't narrow your choice of defendants. In this situation, you should also be suing the busboy, the waiter or waitress (not to mention those at nearby tables), the chef, the maitre d', the bartender, the washroom attendant, the coat-check person, and the parking valet.

If you're the type who just doesn't get sick no matter what you eat, here's some more food for thought. You can sue restaurants who discriminate against adults by offering children's menus. On the other hand, restaurants are obligated to offer early bird specials. To do otherwise would discriminate against those who can't bear to pay retail for a meal.

Dress codes in restaurants have been found to be both discriminatory and a violation of the First Amendment. What you wear makes a statement about you and is protected by the Constitution. When the maitre d' tells you, "No shirt, no shoes, no service," serve him with a lawsuit.

A restaurant also has a duty to warn. There must be written warnings that ordering french fries smothered with melted cheese may result in extra calories. Furthermore, if a waiter or waitress fails to warn you that bleu cheese dressing is fifty cents extra, you can sue your server and the restaurant. They must also warn not to lick the plate, since you may burn your tongue.

When you eat out, you can choose from a menu of lawsuits. You can sue if your meal is too hot, too cold, too spicy or not spicy enough. Unless your meal is just right, your attorney can find just the right lawsuit. A similar suit was brought over an improperly heated bowl of porridge in the case of Goldilocks versus The Three Bears.

We haven't even mentioned the lawsuits you can file against bars. Since a person under the influence cannot think clearly, you are not responsible for any of your actions while drinking. This principle was upheld in Crazy Guggenheim versus Joe the Bartender and Otis versus the Mayberry Diner. At a minimum, the bar should write off your bar tab, since they have no business serving to someone who's visibly intoxicated.

You'll be high on life, once you start suing.

Chapter Twelve

I Am Not An Animal.
I Am A Litigant.

Few people are aware that animals are allowed to sue to remedy injustices. This right to sue grew out of the animal rights movement.

Naturally, animals aren't permitted to sue anyone they want. This would be silly. After all, the courts are crowded enough without every farm animal suing, because the milker's hands are too cold.

If an animal wants to sue, a guardian must be appointed for it. After all, it would be a mockery of justice to allow animals into the courtroom. Who would clean up after them? In addition, how would you tell them apart from the lawyers?

The ground-breaking case involving animals was Mr. Ed versus Wilbur. Mr. Ed was awarded millions in damages, after a jury found Wilbur cheated him out of his residuals.

On appeal, however, the damage award was reduced to a few cubes of sugar. Many legal experts believe Mr. Ed's attorney, Francis, the talking mule, made an ass out of himself in handling the case.

Animals can sue for a variety of reasons. A dog can sue because of the adverse effects of passive smoke. Sometimes, hanging one's head out the window just isn't enough.

Canines can sue their owners for failure to buckle their seatbelts. Even dumb animals know better than that. Several states have passed laws, making it mandatory for pets to be strapped into a car seat. Since dogs don't have thumbs, they are not legally responsible for buckling up themselves.

Dogs can also sue for intentional infliction of emotional distress, if their owners dress them up in those funny little outfits. This can make pets confused about their sexual orientation.

There is also evidence that intelligent dogs can become schizophrenic through improper training methods. This is grounds for a lawsuit, even though the dog is clearly incompetent to testify because of the mental defect.

There are labor laws that protect animals too. Guard dogs and seeing eye dogs must be paid at the minimum wage or greater. They are entitled to at least two breaks per shift. Dogs used to sniff out explosives and drugs must be given hazardous duty pay.

They also are covered by workers' comp and their pensions are guaranteed by the government. Animals in petting zoos are entitled to a percentage of the gross and are eligible for salary arbitration after three years.

Any type of animal can sue for false imprisonment, if forced to travel via airplane in a cage. To avoid a lawsuit, these animals should be upgraded to coach wherever possible. In addition, frequent flyer programs aren't allowed to discriminate against animals making flights.

Animals can also file a civil action for assault, where warranted. Otherwise, a dog could be struck on the nose at will with a newspaper. A dog shocked by an invisible fence can sue the person who installed it.

Some of these lawsuits will be seeking more than just money. A cat can sue to force its owner to change the kitty litter more often. A canary can demand a fresh newspaper to line the bottom of the cage.

Animal testing is strictly prohibited, unless it's cholesterol or SATs.

Pets can sue for invasion of privacy when a photograph is taken of them without getting a release signed.

A prissy French poodle can sue, if the neighbor's St. Bernard has his way with her. Nonetheless, they can utilize "the bitch was asking for it" defense.

But along with the right to sue, animals lose their traditional immunity from litigation. You can sue a dog for sexual harassment for hugging your leg without permission. Woof means no.

In exchange for this right to sue, animals have given up their immunity from suit.

Of course, since most animals except for those that do beer commercials are usually short on cash, they'll need to buy liability insurance. The same companies that offer health insurance for pets are now selling pet liability policies.

These policies are good for everyone, including the insurance industry. It has opened up a whole new market for insurance agents to bore and creates customers by the litter.

Suppose your dog messes up the new rug. It's not enough to scold him. That really accomplishes nothing, since the dog can't remember what he did to deserve a scolding and it certainly doesn't clean your rug.

If your dog is insured, suing is the answer. The dog's policy pays the damages. And when his premium is jacked up at the time of renewal, your dog will get the message that it's wrong to do his business on the rug.

Obviously, there are some problems with these policies. Cats find it hard enough to stay awake, without hearing a pitch from an insurance agent. Furthermore, there are actuarial problems because of the cat's nine lives. Similarly, most actuaries find it tough to crunch the numbers for dogs. They get stuck when it's time to convert dog years into human ones and vice-versa.

Once the bugs are worked out, however, suing can become a way of life for men, women and man's best friends.

Chapter Thirteen

Suit Yourself

Throughout this book, we have discussed every possible person you might sue in the event you're injured. We have come to the conclusion that every injury must be somebody's fault.

In the unlikely event that there's no one to sue, you must seek the ultimate solution. As a last resort, you must consider suing yourself.

Let's say you're having your morning coffee. You take a sip but there's one problem. You poke yourself in the eye with the coffee stirrer.

Obviously, you're not going to sue yourself first. Initially, you'll proceed against the coffee manufacturer for failing to warn you of this danger, not to mention Juan Valdez. If that action fails, however, you must be willing to sue yourself.

Although there have been few lawsuits in this area to date, it will only be a matter of time until the courts are filled with cases of this type. To do otherwise would punish you for your own mistakes and that's just not right. It's not fair for you to lose your right to sue, just because you messed up and hurt yourself accidentally.

For years you've let potential lawsuits like this slip through your fingers. How many times have you spilled food on your lap and thought you had no recourse? Or hit yourself with a hammer? Or fell off a ladder? Or run into a door? Or stuck yourself with a needle? Or sawed off your finger while cutting cheese?

You'll be more careful next time, if your stupidity results in a lawsuit. Imagine being able to sue every time you hit your crazy bone. Be aware, however, that you'll need a medical expert to testify as to the extent of your injury, preferably one who knows the medical term for crazy bone.

Even though you can sue yourself, no court will allow recovery for an intentional act of self-mutilation. Obviously, this might open the door for fraudulent lawsuits which we abhor.

Your insurance company will fully investigate the facts to make certain that the damages are genuine and did result exclusively from your own stupidity.

Dragging yourself through the civil court system can be a harrowing experience. Even though you may negligently injure yourself on more than one occasion, a lawsuit of this type should only be used selectively. You may find that your homeowners insurance policy is cancelled because of these lawsuits.

The preferable strategy is to find someone else with insurance who can be sued. If they don't have insurance, he or she should have the financial resources to cover the huge verdict that you're likely to win.

You don't have anything to lose. Your attorney will handle this matter on a contingency basis. It is called a contingency fee, because a contingent of attorneys could split it and live comfortably on the proceeds forever.

Chapter Fourteen

Conclusion

As with any service, there is no guarantee of success. Nevertheless, your lawyer will make every effort to see that you get your share of the litigation jackpot. And if all else fails, hire another attorney to sue that incompetent shyster for legal malpractice.

When the economy is bad, you have to make money somehow. And lawsuits are the answer. Gee whiz, lawyers have been doing it for years.

The previous chapters have only scratched the surface. We didn't talk at all about the rights of the unborn, the unwashed, the uncola, and the undead. We haven't even mentioned the growing number of lawsuits against inanimate objects.

While offering instruction on legitimate lawsuits, we must chastize those who bring absurd cases to court. We've all read about silly suits such as the woman who claimed she lost her psychic powers as a result of a CAT scan. Any layperson should realize it was probably some other aspect of her medical treatment that caused her to lose those psychic powers. For example, it wouldn't be unusual for a man to lose his psychic powers during a prostate exam.

The practical ramifications of lawsuits should also be noted. There are those physicians who will violate their Hippocratic oath by refusing to treat you, just because you've sued them two or three times. You also may find an occasional friend or relative who is touchy, just because you've named him in a lawsuit. Some may even go to the extreme of taking you off their Christmas card list or won't invite you to their daughter's wedding. There is really no remedy for those petty individuals who will take these matters personally.

It's all part of life and that's why you need this instruction book. Otherwise, you might waste a lifetime, without suing anyone.

Remember:
Life is a lawsuit
waiting to happen!

About The Author

Les Abromovitz is the author of *Taking A Year Off From Work* (1994, J. Flores Publications, Miami) and *Family Insurance Handbook* (1990, McGraw-Hill, New York). He is the managing editor of *Business Insurance Guide* (1993, Summers Press, Austin). His book of personal finance tips, *Money For Nothing, Tips For Free* was recently published by Great Quotations Publishing Company, Glendale Heights, Illinois.

Les and his wife, Hedy, are co-authors of *Bringing TQM On The QT To Your Organization* (1993, SPC Press, Knoxville). They split their time between Pittsburgh and Boca Raton. He is a member of the Pennsylvania Bar and the American Bar Association.

OTHER TITLES BY GREAT QUOTATIONS PUBLISHING COMPANY

GREAT QUOTATIONS PUBLISHING CO.

1967 Quincy Court
Glendale Heights, IL 60139-2045
Phone (708) 582-2800
FAX (708) 582-2813